A LAZY POET

Anda Damisa

© **2019** Anda Damisa
ISBN: 978-978-57291-5-3

No part of this publication may be reproduced, distributed or transmitted in any form or by any means, including photocopying, recording or other electronic or mechanical method, without the prior written permission of the publisher.

Published in Nigeria by:

Daneliherald Communications
Plot 15 Block B Road 411, OPIC Estate, Agbara
www.printdoctorafrica.com | 07030465088

DEDICATION

This collection of poems is dedicated to the

captain of my soul.

ACKNOWLEDGMENT

I would love to appreciate everyone who encouraged me and contributed one way or the other to my growth as a writer and the successful completion of this illustrious work especially my friends at NaijaStories.com. Thank you.

Table of Contents

FOREWORD

Anderson has a radiant soul, evident in this eclectic collection of poems. The author meticulously knitted forcible words the way a priest prays the rosary with élan.

He deftly explores diverse interesting themes with riveting narratives that bring fresh perspectives to fore on the issues of life.

The author bandaged the sutures of age long adventures with the theatrics of new ones.

I commend his effort to have devotedly made this masterpiece available against all odds.

I hope the therapeutic essence of this book does to all the readers, the actual intent of the writer.

Oloyede Michael Taiwo,

Curator, Lagospoetrython.

PREFACE

I am excited to finally share this dream of mine with you. Growing up as an avid reader and a writer, my dream was to have my books in libraries and bookshelves across the country and even though this dream is finally coming true much later than I anticipated, I am still very much excited to have finally taken this first step into the journey of being an author.

Most of the poems you will read in these books were written either from experience or from stories read. I feel like my collection of poetry is something every poetry lover and non-lovers of poetry will be able to relate to as I see my work of poetry as music to the soul. It's simple lines and rhymes, the stories in between, of heartbreak, of love, of pain, of rejection and much more.

There is something for everyone in the pages of this book and I am certain that before you get to the last page of this book, you will have found that one piece of poetry that speaks personally to you.

I am grateful to everyone who has encouraged me to share this book with the world, every poem here was written between 2013 and 2016 and but for those good friends who have pushed me, motivated me and helped to get this started, I would probably have always had this somewhere where I read it to myself when I am bored. I hope you find a piece that sings to your soul and inspires you.

A lazy poet

A BOY'S PRAYER

"If a child washes his hands, he could eat with kings"

- Anonymous

As I face another day

Watch over me Lord when I play

Help me not to cry when I fall

Shine on me your sweetest love

Fill my heart with your truth

As I soon become a youth

Teach me not to steal

Nor to lie

Take me to your bosom,

There, let me lie

Help me to always read and write

So I can grow to be famous, rich and wise

I want to be the best I can

I want to grow into a great man

Hear my pleas when I pray

Lest bad friends lead me astray

Help my friends who steal and fight

Help us tell the wrong from the right

Bless my father

Fill him with strength

Bless my mother

See her through the years

Fill me with laughter

Confront my fears

Make me ONE among my peers

Watch over me when I sleep

In your arms, my soul I keep

Make my life a fairy tale

Happy and sweet this I pray

UPON MY PATH

Commit to the Lord whatever you do, and he will establish your plans - Proverbs 16:3

Lighten my path, oh lord

That I may journey this world with ease

Erase my past

That I may walk beside you in peace

Make my sail smooth and plain

Take me on to a higher plane

When I sleep

Wake me up

When I slip

Refill my cup

These shadows I see through the panes

Take them away and help overcome its pains

Help me believe

And in you only, trust

Be my guide, my light, my beacon

Upon my path

I seek your eyes

Within my heart

I seek your light

Can't journey this world alone

Don't leave me fragile and error prone

Make me honest, steadfast and just

That I may wholeheartedly fulfill your cause

Lighten my path

Night and day

Let me revel in this art

Dwell in you till my dying days

TEACH ME

*"Live as if you were to die tomorrow. Learn as if you
were to live forever" – Gandhi*

"Live as if you were to die tomorrow. Learn as

if you were to live forever" – Gandhi

For wisdom, for knowledge

I hunger. Earnestly, I yearn

Teach me

Let me from childhood learn

Don't blame the government

And their promises never kept

Forget the classrooms

They are just walls

We can learn anywhere

The future knocks

There's a feverish revolution

A goldmine called education

They say the place is called school

I hear, there, men are made

There, dreams come true

For me, anywhere will do

Teach me under the scorching sun

Let it dry my throat

Let it sting through my patched pants

Let me sit upon tree trunks

And get bitten by soldier ants

If the rain falls

We'll hide under the mango tree

I will listen

I will learn

I will read

Teach me without cease

Let my slate be full

I'll read, wipe and write again

Don't just fill my rumbling bowel

Fill my thoughts

Fill it with knowledge

Daily, I hear the stories

Of men who rose from grass to great glory

Teach me

I want to read

I want to write

I want to grow

To be wealthy and wise

Teach me

So tomorrow, my bare feet will wear a shoe

And my lanky frame, a proper cloth

So I can build for my village, many schools

And even for my country, better roads

A lazy poet

A NAIRA

Today's newspaper is tomorrow suya wrapper

- African Proverb

If you are ever lost

For a Naira

You must bear the cost

Rise up determined, work harder

If you persist

And poverty insists

Do not despair

Toil, the harvest you will surely bear

If you are ever stuck

Your dreams lie fallow

Your visions never seem to work

Look with hope to the morrow

Do not falter

Do not stomp

For every hard work, there's a reward

When the going gets tough
This journey of life seem rough
Tread slow and steady
Be at alert, always ready
For opportunity comes in seasons
Its treasures revealed to only those who seize it

Lay your youth not to waste
For but once only
You shall have its taste
Play the world your harmonious flute
Then watch it swoon in your vibrant youth

Be strong, wise and comely
Eventually, you shall find your calling.
Walk not in the ways of the dark
Hide not evil in your heart

Let your ways be moral and just
Stay clear of thugs, guns and drugs
For sooner or later,

The one who kills
Will by the gun, also be killed

Flee, lest your body be defiled
Don't let your bottom lead you along in life
Don't be a failure
A model of dishonor

Do not fret
Do not worry
Never let your faith rest
Or go weary

Stand tall
Believe in your call
For sooner or later
Those who succeed are those who believe
Those who rise from the bruises of a thousand
falls.

A lazy poet

A GREAT POET

"The greatest religions convert the world through stories"
- Ben Okri

I congratulate you great poet

For winning the prized Nobel laureate

You told me poetry beckoned

Then, I asked how

You told me you were determined to till

Drown yourself in the puddles of your ink

Until the hungry world has had its fill

And every nation peace

You fought bravely and you won

With a pen

No gun, no sword

No arsenal of atomic bombs

Now, at every corner
Your carefully crafted words have become a
song
It is sung on the streets
Chanted as a prayer
Other times, accompanied with drama and
melodious beats

Your poems are recited with pride at state
functions and parade grounds
To princes and princesses before they are sleep
bound
Even the poetry hater's children read them at
school
Its wise lines, a medicine for fools

Within its lush pages
Full of gold lettering
No one can see the shadows

When you wrote deep into the night
Under the watchful gaze of the full moon
The whispers of the wind and the chirping
crickets, your company

No one was there when you were stung by the
soldier ants
While you wrote under that large Iroko tree
behind papa's barn
Now your poetry is no longer written on that
tattered notebook you cherished so much
The one papa bought for you when he went up
north
But on fine paper
Made from the family of the same Iroko tree
you used to sit under

They say "poetry saves a nation"
Yours have sparked widespread revolutions
You are a beacon for poetry lovers

A puzzle for poetry haters

Though you were afar, I watched

That old television set at our neighbors

The pictures blurred

Only shades of black and white shown

Still, heard your every word

My heart lurched to your every emotion

When you rose to receive your award

The world saw you cry

No one knew the tortuous road you journeyed

How you persisted

And believed in the power of poetry

I vividly remember

While my fingers were still soft and tender

Yours were already a glowing ember

Lighting up the path to emancipation

You were carefully mastering the art of words

While your mates kicked balls under the sun

Now you are an award-winning poet

Do you know I still battle with metaphors and

sonnets?

Your voice echo nigh brother

Through the burning Sahara

High across the hills of the Fouta D'jalon

Down to the stream that flows behind mama's

farm

A great éclat feverishly resonates

Kings whisper your name

Men applaud with pride

Women await your return

Hoping you will want a bride

I bear our family name like a crown

Your anticipated return peeves the town

Promise me brother

To bring me a pen

That which you used in your quest to conquer

the world

Bring me an exercise book too

So I can make of them a tool

As I explore my creative muse

Congratulations brother

From one poetry lover

To an award winning poet

POKE ME

*Pain is the breaking of the shell that encloses your
understanding. - Kahlil Gibran*

How slow time passes by when you are in pain
Life's subtle mockery

I stare into nothingness all day
Trying to come to term
That you could leave without saying goodbye

I sit from dawn till dusk
Poring over your Facebook page
Hoping you would upload your Status
So I can at least know *what's on your mind*

But alas! Your mind is somewhere else
Where is that place you have gone to
Where there are no phones and internet
connections

Where is that place you have gone to
Where you can't Tweet so I can know what you
are up to

They say you went on an eternal journey
Who embarks on a journey without a mobile
phone
I'm scared and can't tell anyone my best friend
has abandoned me

I keep waking up to hear you call my name
When I ask
They say you are gone
Is that true!
Is it possible to be young, full of strength and
vigor and still die!

I want to think this is all a dream
The emptiness within says otherwise
I need you more than ever
These fresh memories can't fill this deep
vacuum

Your photos and videos only make me want to
hold you
I want to smack you
So you will chase me round and round like you
always do
Maybe
Just maybe
If we keep running
Death won't be able to catch you

Death….
A life ended when it hasn't even begun
How could death betray such youth

I will pick out your diary
One by one, I will write out your plans
Your dreams and your visions
I will place it instead of flowers by your
graveside
So death will be ashamed
When it sees the glory it hassled out of this
arena called life

I miss you

It hurts that I can't call you when next I go to watch a football match

It hurts when you don't reply my Tweets

It hurts to write on your Wall and not get a reply

I just poked you now and I am going to bed

If you truly care

You feel my pains

You see my tears

Poke me in return so I know you are safe where you are

Poke my ribs if you can't poke my Wall

Poke me in my dreams

Poke me anywhere you want

I won't argue and I won't fight

I promise I won't poke you in return.

Just please poke me one more time

I love you friend, brother and everything else you are but never got the chance to be.

DO NOT LOVE ME

The heart was made to be broken

- Oscar Wilde

Do not love me

Do not care

This heart has nothing to share

Do not tempt me with the allure of your lips

What would a kiss do?

But for a while, set my troubles at ease

Do not dare to tease me

For I am lost to passion

Don't try to set my mind at ease

I am not yours to nurture

Pain has numbed me

Its poison flows through my veins

I am empty, broken and lost

My heart, a cobweb of sutures

Many have tried

To tame this heart you crave

My fingers are numb

How could they touch?

Unleash the treasures of your luscious limbs

They hold no warmth to arouse your thrusting
nips

My vile tongue holds no words to charm

Nor songs of poetry to bring you bliss

Do not tease me with the wiggle of your waist

For therein, I will only be lost for a day

I have trust only in the fire of my thrust

I will torch your groin with the brute of a savage

Still by dawn, I will be gone

Your loins filled with yearning that will never
age

Do not try to know me
I am nought but mystery
Burnt and untamed

Do not trust me
I am nought but fleeting
A roaming stray

I roam a place unseen
In a cloak of broken dreams
This wound you can't mend
Do not love me
Do not care
All it will bring you is despair.

A lazy poet

A HEART APART

"All souls are lost until they are found."
- Kate McGahan

Who will tame this heart

This beast that beats from the rest apart

Who can dance to this unique song

That which slips unrequited off my cultured

tongue

From whence will that one come

That who will strut and with me prance

Make this feisty heart throb at first glance

She who will taste of the kisses of my lips

And remain whole

She who will move to the rhythm of my hips

And bring forth the allures of a home

Beauties I have come across in my sojourn

Like a tempestuous wind

Many have fallen to my coated sting

Can love then make of me a new-born

Then for love I wait

For every that I have come across

Are to my lust, just slaves

Slaves to the innate skills of my manly thrust

Let love close the fleeting shutters

of my roving eye

Let love douse my fiery flames

On its sensuous wings, let me fly

Let love engulf me and snare my being

in cupid's chain

Let me find she whom my heart beats for

And in her arms be tamed

Let love forever binds this heart

Let love quench my hunger in her dainty charms

YOUNG MAIDEN

*You may be one person to the world but you may also be
the world to one person*

- Audrey Hepburn

Oh fair skinned beauty

Why do you prance around like a wayward
chicken?

See your soft skin glow

With the sheen luster of many diamond stones

When you walk

Your twin fawns mercilessly bounce

Its ample bulk convey a communal dance

Its proud nip thrusting forth like a royal crown

See your luscious backside sway

Like two halves of the moon on ethereal display

When you dance

Your bare feet trots, a song

Of its own, it beat an adjoining sound

A rhythm sweeter than the melody of many
talking drums

I feel a heat rise off your supple hips

Piping hot seduction

The colorful beads they wear

Hold the silent promise of a fertile line

I feel the sensuousness of your sultry lips

Soft with the lure of freshly tapped palm wine

Fill this warrior's heart

Oh young maiden

Quench my virile desires

So heavy laden

Open to me the treasures of your mind

Let me take you, teach you

Tame you with my cultured fingers, nimble and
wise

THE GOLDEN QUARTET

"Sex is an emotion in motion."

- Mae West

Light wind steadily blew

Waves rolled, crashing rocks in strokes of beau

Nuts struck

Palms bowed to the beauty of the setting sun

A feet-empty beach beckoned

With grace she swayed

Music emanated of the beads that adorned her
waist

Her bare feet she flayed

And when she turned to smile

Pent up feelings went astray

Her fingers touched

I put my lips to hers

Therein I became cursed

Hungrily I kissed
I wined and sipped
Till of her twin fawn I became drunk
I swooned in her mien, love some

I yearned for more
I touched, touched and touched again
I curled lines across her sensuous planes
Upon her skin, I drew maps of lost empires
I carved out new states
I mapped out strategies to conquer every part of
her womanly curves

Again, she touched me
Pulses went awry
Engulfed, I got lost in her searing heat
In unison, I felt our heart beat
Clothings dropped, slinked off in defeat

We danced until we got lost in our
own grinding beat

Trapped in the threshold of pleasure

We feasted on its bouquet without measure

Then, her heart called and I took her

I bit her nip and she moaned a rousing song of

want and desire

We danced and twirled in churning beauty

Painting on the sands, every lovers fantasy

When eventually we met

Lightning sparked, raindrops came down in

rousing descent

Time stopped in testament to that golden

moment

When love, sex, moonlight and the water

quartet merged as one

A lazy poet

THIS WOMAN

"The black woman is the most unprotected, unloved woman on earth…she is the only flower on earth that grows unwatered.

– Malcolm X

She moves in silky steps
Her mien carves out treacherous lines, dainty sonnets
Her wiggling waist weaves romantic poems.

When she dances
Her bare feet raise dust from the brown earth
They hang over her
Stuck in awe
A testament to her prowess

The beads of her waist jingle
They sing a song of their own
They tell a tale often untold
Like rainbow, their beauty shone
Colorful, proud and bold

Upon her lips
Courage sings
None rivals the tenacity of her words
Her allure screams
Her sonorous sound, a bond

Her twin fawns stand tall
Rising and falling with the beat of her thumping
heart
Tiny rivulets of sweat hang upon her forehead
Adding luster to sheen unseen

Her arms moves swiftly with her leaping steps
Her sagging back, a tower of strength
Though weary
The gleam in her eyes never darken

This woman
Of her grace, comely
Her aura, loving
Men of valor are made

THE COBBLER

A shoe has so much more to offer than just to walk

- Christian Louboutin

I have traversed many lands

Learning a trade for my nimble hands

Some call me the magic cobbler

Some, the great shoe maker

I will frame the sole of your feet

Carve you a shoe that perfectly fits

Of the finest of rare leathers

With the wondrous delight of assorted feathers

Let me see your stubborn sole

Tame it with a shoe that sings to the soul

Let my fingers sow and weave

Till it brings you soothing bliss

I will cut you a colorful skin

Taut with a glowing sheen

I see your shoe lacks that touch

That of a master to make it gleam

I will make you a perfect shoebox

Of the finest of cedar and soft perfume

After a fancy catwalk

It will keep your shoes in its bloom

Call me the magic cobbler

Call me the great shoemaker

I make shoes that brings smiles

And helps you sail easy through this life.

LAGOS TAXI DRIVER

*There used to be a strong belief that if you wanted to
know what was really going on in a country, the best
thing to do was to go there and ask a taxi driver*

- Michael Korda

Under the scorching eye of the Lagos sun

I labor daily, from dusk to dawn

Driving through my jolly city

Cursing and weaving through its heaving traffic

I pick bankers, musicians,

Sometimes, actors and physicians

Even lawyers and reluctantly, politicians

The last promised I will head all cab drivers

If I carried his posters around till the elections
are over

Now I see him only when I'm home to watch
the news

One year gone, almost two

I once met a rapper

He had hair like palm trees at Tinapa

I had to put on a frown

So I wouldn't laugh at the ugly clown

Last week, I picked my last prophet

He left me with no money and a lot of
pamphlets

The walls of this cab hold many stories

It's worn out seats, a creased mystery

I once picked two lovers

From Banana island down to Ikeja

They defiled my taxi

Made me so horny

We almost crashed off the Third mainland
bridge

I love riding through the Island

Crisscrossing the many flyovers

While staring past the elegant skyscrapers

I sometimes have lunch by the bar beach
When I'm happy and want to pretend I am rich
I pick the market women too
From Ebute Meta most times to Mile 2
I'm content with what I do
Cruising this town
Learning its nooks

I am over forty
Seasoned and plucky
Nothing makes me feel better
Than being a Lagos taxi driver

A lazy poet

A NEW ANTHEM

If corruption had already taken root, then good seeds
must be preserved

- Toba Beta

See how you loudly prattle

In a mishmash of assorted preambles

Your bulging belly, wrestles to be free

Your smile, fickle, ready to flee

You prance around in garland of excess
brocades

Waving your wand of stolen Naira, a tempting
bait

When you parade that podium

To mime your stale and lofty speech

Do you not think of birthing freedom?

Finding a noose to hang poverty, lest it chokes
us

You sing of building good roads and a million
bridges
Schools made of sweets and regular electricity

Oh! The depth of your boring manifesto
The barren ethos of your shallow ego
You swear to uphold the law
Yet you tar only those roads to the doorstep of
your many in-laws

Drink, dance, and eat all you can
For I hear the anthem of a new birth
A jury to reveal your mischief
The wail of sirens to mourn your greed
Your tears to heal our scars
Our taxes to put you behind bars
We will burn the flames of a new ember

Until it parachutes us into the dreams of our
heroes' past

54

ON THAT DAY

"Great love and great achievements involve great risks"

\- Dalai Lama

On the day I was born

The wick of a small lamp brightly burned

The rain met the sky with stubborn brute

It beat an anticipating sound on our tin roof

When I silently came

On that cold night in May

I slipped into a waiting arm

My tiny buttocks was firmly spanked

Relentlessly I cried

I was a handful for anyone

Yet hard they tried

No gong announced my entry
No one came dancing with drums and
tambourines
There was no seven-day feast
Just a father's warm smile
A mother's breast milk
A neighbor's palm wine

No one brought me a gift
While I was blissfully asleep
I grew quickly into a man
A destiny drawn through a tortuous path.

On the day you were born
Corporations stood at a stand still
Many prayed
Others paced
While you were eagerly anticipated

When you came

You cried

Screaming orders into the waiting world

Nurses scurried around

Tending to your every jerk of the hand

A week later

Men of eminence gathered

Journalists jostled for space

Cameras pried for a glimpse of your face

Your arrival was greatly heralded

A fanfare gloriously celebrated

The heir to an empire

On the eve of that cold November

Gifts and cars were given to you

Even though your limbs were still soft and new

Your destiny was charted that day

Later arranged and rearranged

Set on a dramatic pathway

A planned future, readymade

On the day our path crossed

We stood high on campaign hills

I strung together elegant words

While you strewn the streets with looted Naira

bills

You waved from the open roof of your Rolls

Royce

While I danced in the city square to my people's

voice

Yours was a grand coronation

Mine, a call for a revolution

You eyed and I smiled

You schemed and I screamed

Your sword was the newspaper and televisions

Mine was a true outline of my great vision

My words burned brightly in their heart

While you're Naira bills was your only pact

On that hot afternoon in March

You knew I was more than just a match

On the day that we met

On the shores of a foreign land

We shook hands

You praised my prowess

You asked how I made it

And I told you of nation building

You asked for the source of my power

And I told you I needed no cabal

You marveled like a new bride

Ready to join the moving tide

On the day we met,

An incumbent president and the next

We streamlined our alliances

Built a better vision for our masses

On the day we met

Our nation started the rise to a towering
crescent

PAIN SONG

"There are wounds that never show on the body that are deeper and more hurtful than anything that bleeds." - Laurell K. Hamilton

I am fettered and bound in chains only I can
feel
I am hunted by an unforgiving past
Assaulted by a future unseen

I trudge through this prison
Bordered in tween
Hopelessness, unreason and maladies deep

This enigma stings me
Its brutal laughter haunts me in the dark
It taunts me with errors past
In its poison, I am lost
My heart tattooed with ugly sutures
My soul wounded, bruised and tortured

This whip of anger and deceit

Brutally cuts deep but never bleeds

Hopelessness holds me hostage

Lies, broken hearts pay me homage

Lost in a bottomless abyss

I carry alone, this burden

Within the walls of this lonely lair

I am subdued, a servant to fear

There, pain rules, a ruthless warden

I sink in its complicity

An unwilling accomplice

I soak its torture

A mocking travesty

Now, I nurture this pain

Its pleasure, ecstasy

I am forever lost in this wasteland

Here, I am stuck and no longer a stranger

My fold and order has crumbled into

nothingness

To this disorder, I have succumbed

I hope to forget my wounds and go numb

I don't want to feel

I don't want to fill

With hope, this heart I have learnt to steel

I have looked farther

No light beckoned

I have screamed Father!

I hear no redemption song

Alone in this wasteland I belong

Writing, crying and withering away to this pain

song

IMPRISONED

"However long the night, the dawn will break"

– African Proverb

In the webs of my past

I roam, imprisoned

Bound in chains of unbelief and unreason

In my inactions and inertia, trapped

Tormenting my soul with its laughter crude

Pain rules, a warden brute

I will sing of this pain

Like a titled mourner's hymn

Though in vain

I curse this searing sting

This pain that has thrust my being

Into willows of epileptic throes

My soul is crippling in arthritic woes

This pain gloats and grows

Though hard I try to drown it

In bottles of intoxicating spirits

Its venom like a strong tide flows

Spilling forth rivulets of insidious stings

GRIEF

No one here gets out alive

- Jim Morrison

How can I live

With pain this grave

How can I grieve

With every word, my voice breaks

My soul is numb

Tears have ceased

My breath falters

This heart creaks

I have embraced liquor

In its berth, I have drowned

Hoping I'd find succor

Yet, its solace eludes me

Peace mocks me

Its silence, mean

A soundless brute, searing through my being

My being, death has conquered

You have made me empty, a man shattered

Now I leave

In search of a titled mourner

To help share my grief.

THE STORM

Each time dawn appears, the mystery is there in its entirety

\- Rene Daumal

The heavily pregnant clouds smile

Thunder bolts accompanied it with roaring laughter

Piercing lightning raged

Contributing its own to their excited chatter

They argued, agreed and disagreed

Together they threw tantrums

Tearing into the inky night

Each showing untamed might.

Lightning struck,

Thunder in return beat its drums

The pregnant cloud rumbled and raged

Till water broke

Its underbelly overflowed

Pouring down in blinding showers

Filling pots and earthenware

Watering gardens and waking sleeping flowers.

The earth opened it pores

To drink, soak and store

The wind whistled by defiantly

Ruffling the plants

Cooling the leaves

Swaying the wet and tired leaves.

As its torrents slowly eased

The heavens coughed

Shaking off the stormy contortions

The pleased rainbow slipped out teasingly

Spreading out its dappled beauty

And staking its claim across the chilly skies

FAREWELL

"How lucky I am to have something that makes saying
goodbye so hard."

-   A.A. Milne

Dance, beautiful bride

Dance, till the gods declare a feast

Let them hear that song your nimble feet sing

Let the earth whisper to the heaven in gossip

"No one ever twirled upon me with such bliss"

My daughter of wonder

You that ease my face of its wrinkles

You that fill my age with virgin chuckles

My frail bones are strengthened by your warmth

Now, my winters are colorful verses ushering in

the summer

With vigor, your womb shall boom
In the harvest, it shall bloom

You will find succor in the arms of your man
Solace in the cuddle of your children
Wondrous music in the scream of many
grandchildren

I can't stop this river of aches
I smile though my heart strains

Sing for me my favorite song
Let it ease my pain when you are gone
Let it echo at the dawn of the morrow and
beyond
When you journey forth to make yourself a new
home